THE PASSION OF THE CHRIST

THE PASSION OF THE CHRIST

EIGHT STUDIES ON THE CROSS

Authentic

First published 2005 by Authentic Media
9 Holdom Avenue, Bletchley, Milton Keynes, Bucks, MK1 1QR, UK
and 129 Mobilization Drive, Waynesboro, GA 30830-4575, USA
www.authenticmedia.co.uk

British Library Cataloguing in Publication Data
A catalogue record for this book is available from the British Library

ISBN 1-85078-385-3

Cover design by Phil Houghton
Typeset by Temple Design
Print Management by Adare Carwin
Pinted and bound by J. H. Haynes & Co. Ltd., Sparkford

CONTENTS

ABOUT THIS BOOK

The Passion of the Christ is a thought-provoking film for Christians and those interested in the Christian faith. The aim of this study guide is to provide a forum in which you can discuss the film and delve more deeply into the issues it raises. This book is intended primarily for a group situation, but can easily be used by individuals as a personal study.

FOR GROUP MEMBERS

It would be helpful if all the group members had seen the film although it is not essential as only the TAKE 2 sections relate directly to it.

You will probably get more out of the study if you spend some time during the week thinking about the study questions and looking up the Bible references. Make a note of your thoughts to share with the group.

Pray that God would teach you what he wants you to learn from the study and that he'd show you how to apply it.

Bring a Bible with you to the session.

FOR INDIVIDUALS

Although this book was written primarily for groups it can easily be used by individuals.

You will not have the benefit of a group to discuss the film or the LIFE FOCUS sections with, but take time to consider your own answers and talk through your thoughts with a friend or prayer partner.

Try to write down your answers for the WHAT DOES THE BIBLE SAY? sections as putting pen to paper will help you clarify your thoughts and think through the issues.

INTRODUCTION

Around AD 30, on a hill outside Jerusalem a man died. The Romans thought they were executing a troublemaker; the Jewish leaders thought they were extinguishing the latest religious fanatic upsetting the status quo and threatening to topple them from power. Only a few people recognised that this man was different. Only a few believed his claim to be the Son of God, the Messiah promised in the Scriptures.

The authorities and even his closest friends thought his death would be the end, but in many ways it was just the beginning. Three days later he rose from the dead as he had promised. And when he ascended into heaven his power was spectacularly released to his disciples. The results were astounding. His followers multiplied, his teachings spread and were recorded, the miracles continued. His radical message changed lives.

But of all the words he spoke and the wonders he performed it is his death which defines history. His death has had more influence than all the politicians that have ever lived or all the teachers who have ever taught. Crucifixion was a crude way to die, the cruellest mankind could devise. Later generations have tried to glamorise his death and minimise its effects but the passing years, and the multitude of cynics, have done nothing to lessen its power. Jesus' death demonstrated a love people had never witnessed before and offered a forgiveness they could never earn. In a miraculous way the death of Jesus of Nazareth has brought life to millions – and still does.

THE SEARCH FOR TRUTH

Jesus: *'All men who hear the truth hear my voice.'*
Roman Governor: *'Truth! What is truth?'*

THE BIG IDEA

Pilate, the Roman Governor, was ahead of his time. He asked one of the most common questions of the post-modern generation – 'What is truth?' The dilemma was that Pilate had his truth; the religious leaders and the crowds had theirs. They had their own beliefs and their own perception of reality and then Jesus arrived announcing that not only his words but he himself was absolute truth. The response then was the same as it is today – a few accepted his radical claim that he was the only way to God; some found his claims absurd; still others found him offensive, worthy of death.

Ask yourself…

If you had been alive in Jerusalem during Passion Week do you think you would have accepted the truth about Jesus?

TAKE 2

Pilate: *'What is truth, Claudia? Do you hear it, recognise it when it is spoken?'*

His wife: *'Yes, I do. Don't you?'*

Pilate: *'How? Can you tell me?'*

His wife: *'If you will not hear the truth, no one can tell you.'*

- What struck you from the film about the following people's reactions to Jesus? Why do you think they were so opposed to him and what he stood for?
  - the religious leaders
  - the crowd
  - the soldiers
  - the Roman governor

WHAT DOES THE BIBLE SAY?

1 Throughout the gospels Jesus is recorded as saying 'I tell you the truth...' What is Jesus' truth concerned with? Look up John 3:3, 5; 5:19, 24; 6:32; 8:58 for example.

2 Christianity claims that Jesus not only spoke the truth but is the truth (John 1:14, 17; 14:6). What does this mean?

3 If God is truth what does this tell us about his activity in the world? Look at John 17:17; Psalm 96:13; Job 37:16.

4 What does a God of truth demand of his followers? Look up Exodus 20:16, Psalm 51:6, John 4:23–24, 16:13, Ephesians 4:15. Paraphrase these verses to help you better understand what God requires.

5 Read John 8:32–36 below. Describe the freedom that truth brings.

> *32'Then you will know the truth, and the truth will set you free.'*
>
> *33They answered him, 'We are Abraham's descendants and have never been slaves of anyone. How can you say that we shall be set free?'*
>
> *34Jesus replied, 'I tell you the truth, everyone who sins is a slave to sin. 35Now a slave has no permanent place in the family, but a son belongs to it forever. 36So if the Son sets you free, you will be free indeed.'*

LIFE FOCUS

Jesus: *'You believe in me. You know that I am the Way, the Truth, and the Life. And no one comes to the Father but by me.'*

- Why do Christians not always feel free in the sense that Jesus intended? Is there anything we can do to change this?

- Jesus marries absolute truth and freedom. Why does our generation want to sever the link? What are the consequences?

- If it is only believers who hear and understand truth (John 18:37), is there any value in listening to atheist scientists or doctors for example? How can we explain the strands of truth found in the secular world?

- 1 Timothy 3:15 describes the church as 'the pillar and foundation of the truth'. In what areas is the church in danger of jeopardizing the truth? In a church community how can we facilitate truth? Consider how we protect the truths of the gospel as well as preserve integrity and honesty among Christians.

RESPONSE

In twos pray through some of the issues that have arisen from this week's study.

Remember if God is truth then what he says about us must be true. Finish your session together by praising God for the truth about his love for us, the privileged status he has given us and the good plans he has for us. Use these verses and choose songs to help you focus on this theme.

> Psalm 139:13–14 *'You created my inmost being; you knit me together in my mother's womb. I praise you because I am fearfully and wonderfully made.'*
>
> Ephesians 2:6, 7, 10 *'And God raised us up with Christ and seated us with him in the heavenly realms in Christ Jesus in order that in the coming ages he might show the incomparable riches of his grace, expressed in his kindness to us in Christ Jesus. For we are God's workmanship, created in Christ Jesus to do good works, which God prepared in advance for us to do.'*
>
> 1 Peter 2:9 *'But you are a chosen people, a royal priesthood, a holy nation, a people belonging to God, that you may declare the praises of him who called you out of darkness into his wonderful light.'*
>
> 1 John 3:1 *'How great is the love the Father has lavished on us that we should be called children of God.'*

FURTHER STUDY

If you would like to examine more closely the truth of the Christian faith John Blanchard's book *Does God Believe in Atheists* gives a valuable defence of belief in God.

THE PAIN OF SUFFERING

'He was wounded for our transgressions, crushed for our iniquities; by His wounds we are healed.' Isaiah 53

THE BIG IDEA

Jesus' death can become so familiar that we often fail to appreciate the extent of his suffering. We skip over the details in the gospel accounts but the film graphically portrays the horror of those last 24 hours – the anguish of a mother watching her son suffer, unable to stop his pain; the despair of Jesus' followers as they deny him, betray him and watch their hope fade; and the unimaginable spiritual, emotional and physical agony Jesus endured. Historians tell us crucifixion was the cruellest form of death known to mankind – add to that the brutality Jesus suffered before he reached Golgotha, the weight of humanity's sin, and rejection by his heavenly father and we begin to understand the cost of our salvation.

Ask yourself…

What difference does appreciating the extent of Christ's sufferings make to you? Does it help strengthen your faith? Does it help you deal with your own suffering?

TAKE 2

Mary: 'My son ... when, where, how will you choose to be delivered of this?'

- What was your initial response as you watched the tremendous suffering contained in the film? What aspect affected you most?

WHAT DOES THE BIBLE SAY?

1 Who is ultimately responsible for suffering? Look at Job 1:1–12, 2:6; Isaiah 45:7; Amos 3:6; 2 Corinthians 12:7–10.

2 What is the purpose of suffering? Look at the following references to help start your discussion:

> Galatians 6:8
>
> Hebrews 12:4–7
>
> 1 Peter 1:6–7
>
> Psalm 119:67
>
> Job 42:1–6

3 What particular type of suffering and hardship is involved in Christian ministry? Consider the lives of key Bible characters:

> Moses (Numbers 11:13–15)
>
> Jeremiah (Jeremiah 20:7–10)
>
> Paul (2 Corinthians 6:3–10; 11:22–29)
>
> John (Revelation 1:9)

> What do you learn from these men about what to expect and how to respond to suffering?

4 Each of the gospel writers explains the events of Jesus' crucifixion as happening 'so that Scripture might be fulfilled'

(e.g. Matthew 26:54). Look at Psalm 22; Zechariah 11:12; 13:7; and Isaiah 52:13–53:12 – what Old Testament prophecies did Jesus fulfil? What does it mean to you to know that God actually planned Jesus' suffering in advance?

5 Look at Philippians 3:7–11 below. What does it mean to 'share in the sufferings of Christ'? What type of suffering is involved? For some discussion ideas look at Matthew 10:37–39; Acts 5:41; 1 Peter 4:15–16.

> *⁷But whatever was to my profit I now consider loss for the sake of Christ. ⁸What is more, I consider everything a loss compared to the surpassing greatness of knowing Christ Jesus my Lord, for whose sake I have lost all things. I consider them rubbish, that I may gain Christ ⁹and be found in him, not having a righteousness of my own that comes from the law, but that which is through faith in Christ – the righteousness that comes from God and is by faith. ¹⁰I want to know Christ and the power of his resurrection and the fellowship of sharing in his sufferings, becoming like him in his death, ¹¹and so, somehow, to attain to the resurrection from the dead.*

LIFE FOCUS

Jesus: *'My God, My God why have you forsaken me?'*

- If suffering is ultimately from God's hand, is it right to relieve the suffering of others?

- Some people spiritually mature and others crack under the weight of suffering. What factors determine people's response to suffering?

- Describe what a mature Christian's response to suffering should look like. What would you hope their attitude and behaviour to be? What support would you expect them to look for? What focus and priorities would you wish them to have?

- The church has always been intended as a place for people who are hurting and perhaps the needs are greater now than ever before – single mothers, divorced people, families where only one spouse is a believer, etc. How equipped is your church to respond to these needs? What practical action could be taken to help these individuals?

- Consider the various explanations for suffering you discussed above. If you are suffering at the moment can you attribute a biblical explanation to it? How does this help?

RESPONSE

In twos pray through some of the issues that have arisen from this week's study.

After he'd been flogged, Pilate brought Jesus before the crowd and said 'Behold the man!' Finish your session together by doing just that – not focusing on his broken body but on the beauty of his character and what his suffering means to us.

In your worship time you may find it helpful to use the following titles. The religious leaders spoke them mockingly to Jesus but to us they are precious:

'Behold the man'
He is the bread of life
Jesus of Nazareth
The King of the Jews
The Son of God
The Messiah
The Son of the Living God
The Son of David
The great 'I AM'

FURTHER STUDY

C.S. Lewis addresses the issue of suffering in his classic treatise *The Problem of Pain*.

THE POWER OF FORGIVENESS

> Jesus: *'This is my blood of the new covenant which is given for you and for many, for the forgiveness of sins. Do this in memory of me.'*

THE BIG IDEA

At the Last Supper Jesus explained to his disciples the reason for the cross – that it was the only way to forgive sins. They didn't understand what he was saying but, according to the film, perhaps the woman who accompanied his mother to mop up his blood after the flogging understood the need for forgiveness better. The last time this woman had studied the ground so closely was when the religious leaders had hauled her in front of Jesus charged with adultery. They were waiting for him to condemn her, and so was she, but he simply drew in the sand and invited whoever was sinless to cast the first stone. One by one the men dropped their stones on the ground and walked away. Perhaps this woman loved Jesus so much because she knew she had been forgiven much (John 8:1–11).

Ask yourself…

Do you really believe that your sins were serious enough to warrant Jesus' death on the cross?

TAKE 2

Jesus: *'Father, forgive them…for they know not what they do.'*

- How does the film portray the power of forgiveness? Think about:
  - Jesus' attitude and actions
  - Judas' despair when there was no forgiveness
  - the response of the two thieves crucified next to Jesus

WHAT DOES THE BIBLE SAY?

1 Why was death required for the forgiveness of sins and in particular why did it have to be Christ who died? Look below at Hebrews 9:13–14, 22, 25–28.

> *[13]The blood of goats and bulls and the ashes of a heifer sprinkled on those who are ceremonially unclean sanctify them so that they are outwardly clean. [14]How much more, then, will the blood of Christ, who through the eternal Spirit offered himself unblemished to God, cleanse our consciences from acts that lead to death, so that we may serve the living God!*

> *[22]In fact, the law requires that nearly everything be cleansed with blood, and without the shedding of blood there is no forgiveness.*

> *[25]Nor did he (Jesus) enter heaven to offer himself again and again, the way the high priest enters the Most Holy Place every year with blood that is not his own. [26]Then Christ would have had to suffer many times since the creation of the world. But now he has appeared once for all at the end of the ages to do away with sin by the sacrifice of himself. [27]Just as man is destined to die once, and after that to face judgment, [28]so Christ was sacrificed once to take away the sins of many people; and he will appear a second time, not to bear sin, but to bring salvation to those who are waiting for him.*

2 God's forgiveness is a free gift; however, we do have a part to play. Look at the following verses to find out our role and discuss why God makes these requirements of us – Acts 10:43, 20:21; Luke 6:37.

3 Review the following verses. How is the completeness of our forgiveness graphically portrayed? Can you think of any other modern analogies?

　　– Psalm 103:12

　　– Isaiah 38:17, 43:25

　　– Micah 7:19

4 What does the Bible tell us about the extent of God's desire to forgive us? What can you learn from the following references: Luke 23:39–43; Jonah 3:10; 4:1–3, 11.

5 God's forgiveness is conditional upon our repentance. Can we forgive someone if they are unwilling to repent of their sin towards us? See Matthew 6:14; Mark 11:25; Ephesians 4:32.

LIFE FOCUS

Thief on the cross: *'I have sinned, and my punishment is just. You would be justified in condemning me. I ask only that you remember me, Lord, when you enter your kingdom.'*

Jesus: *'Amen, I tell you, on this day you shall be with me in paradise.'*

- Why is the need for forgiveness such a strong human drive? How do our contemporaries seek to ease their consciences?

- Why do you think even Christians find it hard to accept God's forgiveness? What can we do to appropriate God's forgiveness fully?

- What difference would it make to your life if you truly appreciated how much you had been forgiven? How would your behaviour, speech and priorities change?

- Unlike God, when humans forgive the memory of the offence still remains. Is complete restoration of a broken relationship ever possible?

- How often do you ask God for forgiveness? How often should you?

RESPONSE

In twos pray through some of the issues that have arisen from this week's study.

Be prepared to act on what you have learnt:

- Do you need to ask God for forgiveness for a specific sin?

- Is there someone you need to forgive?

- Is there a friend or family member you need to ask forgiveness from?

- Do you need to accept God's complete forgiveness so you can live in freedom?

Close your session together by praising God for his priceless forgiveness – the lengths Jesus went to secure it and the vast number of sins it covers.

In the light of this, be gracious with your forgiveness. As Jesus said, 'My command is this: Love each other as I have loved you.' (John 15:12)

FURTHER STUDY

R.T. Kendall wrote his most popular book on this difficult subject. *Total Forgiveness* deals with the challenges and rewards of obeying God and completely forgiving those who have hurt us.

THE PROBLEM OF EVIL

The devil: *'Do you really believe that one man can bear the full burden of sin? No one can carry this burden, I tell you. It is far too heavy. Saving their souls is too costly.'*

THE BIG IDEA

The disciples had been with Jesus three years, they'd heard his teaching, seen his miracles; they were his closest friends. And yet when the end came probably Jesus' most reliable companion was – the devil! When his friends couldn't stay awake the devil was there tempting him in Gethsemane. When they fled in fear the devil stayed to watch the flogging and joined the merciless crowd on the long road to the foot of the cross. To all intents and purposes it looked as if the devil had won, that his plotting and scheming in the hearts of men had paid off – Jesus was dead. But the moment Jesus died Satan's own powers were decisively defeated. What he thought was Jesus' downfall was really his own.

Ask yourself…

To what extent do you think the devil was telling the truth when he said 'No one can carry this burden [of sin]'? What is the evidence in contemporary society that people still struggle with the burden of sin, guilt and shame?

TAKE 2

The devil to Jesus in Gethsemane. *'Who is your father? Who are you?'*

- What did you think of the way the devil was portrayed in the film? What aspects provoked your thinking and challenged you? Were there any aspects of the portrayal you disagreed with? Explain why.

WHAT DOES THE BIBLE SAY?

1 How did the devil and his angels originate? Look at Isaiah 14:12–15. (cf. 2 Peter 2:4; Jude 6).

2 Look up some of the references to the devil. What do his names reveal about his character and the tactics he will employ against us?

- Revelation 12:9, 10
- John 8:44
- 1 John 2:13
- 2 Corinthians 4:4
- Ephesians 2:2
- 1 Peter 5:8

3 What are the particular tactics the devil employs against the church? Look at 2 Corinthians 2:5–11; 11:12–15; 2 Timothy 2:24–26; Revelation 2:10.

4 How should we protect ourselves from the work of the devil? Explain what Ephesians 6:10–18 means for you in your context.

5 What comfort does Malachi 3:14–4:3 offer us?

> *14'You have said, "It is futile to serve God. What did we gain by carrying out his requirements and going about like mourners before the LORD Almighty? 15But now we call the arrogant*

blessed. *Certainly the evildoers prosper, and even those who challenge God escape.*'"

¹⁶*Then those who feared the LORD talked with each other, and the LORD listened and heard. A scroll of remembrance was written in his presence concerning those who feared the LORD and honored his name.*

¹⁷*'They will be mine', says the LORD Almighty, 'in the day when I make up my treasured possession. I will spare them, just as in compassion a man spares his son who serves him.* ¹⁸*And you will again see the distinction between the righteous and the wicked, between those who serve God and those who do not.'*

¹*'Surely the day is coming; it will burn like a furnace. All the arrogant and every evildoer will be stubble, and that day that is coming will set them on fire,' says the LORD Almighty. 'Not a root or a branch will be left to them.* ²*But for you who revere my name, the sun of righteousness will rise with healing in its wings. And you will go out and leap like calves released from the stall.* ³*Then you will trample down the wicked; they will be ashes under the soles of your feet on the day when I do these things,' says the LORD Almighty.*

LIFE FOCUS

Jesus: *'Hear me, Father. Rise up, defend me. Save me from the traps they set for me.'*

- In general, do you think we give the devil too much or too little credit?

- How would you respond to someone who said, 'God can't be good if he allows evil in the world.'

- Throughout the film we see Satan watching Jesus suffer. What difference does it make to know that Satan is watching your suffering?

- How would you respond to someone who believed we are all born good and that it is only a few people who, through lack of love and proper guidance, commit evil acts?

- Share examples of occasions when others have done evil to you. How did you respond? How should Christians respond to evil done to them, even by other Christians? What can we learn from Christ's example?

- What are the issues or areas of life where Satan usually attacks you? Which of his tactics are you particularly susceptible to? How can you better protect yourself against these attacks?

RESPONSE

In twos pray through some of the issues that have arisen from this week's study.

Close your session by reflecting on Christ's decisive victory over Satan on the cross. Choose songs, hymns, prayers and passages of Scripture to read to one another as you focus on this theme. If it is helpful, use the following verse as a starting point for your worship.

'When you were dead in your sins and in the uncircumcision of your sinful nature, God made you alive with Christ. He forgave us all our sins, having cancelled the written code, with its regulations, that was against us and that stood opposed to us; he took it away, nailing it to the cross. And having disarmed the powers and authorities, he made a public spectacle of them, triumphing over them by the cross.' Colossians 2:13–15.

FURTHER STUDY

Michael Green's *I Believe in Satan's Downfall* deals with the biblical accounts of Satan's origin, his strategies and his defeat.

THE SEARCH FOR PURPOSE

Jesus: *'My kingdom is not of this world.'*

Roman Governor: *'Then you are a king.'*

Jesus: *'That is why I was born. To give testimony to the truth.'*

THE BIG IDEA

Throughout history certain men and women have had a keen sense of purpose that has propelled them to greatness. Winston Churchill leading the country to war is a prominent example. We too can experience this sense of purpose when we do what we feel we were created to do – whether it's running, preaching, teaching or being a parent. Jesus explained the purpose for his life to his disciples from their earliest days together but they couldn't comprehend what he was saying. Unlike anyone else in history Jesus' purpose for living culminated in his death; the cross was part of the plan, he knew he had been born to die.

Ask yourself…

What are the main reasons why people today reject Christianity? Is a refusal to accept God's agenda/purpose for their life a key factor?

TAKE 2

Jesus: *'Father, you can do all things. If it is possible, let this chalice pass from me…But let your will be done, not mine.'*

- As you reflect on the film, what purposes motivated the actions and attitudes of each of these groups or individuals?
    - Jesus
    - Pilate
    - religious leaders
    - the disciples
    - Simon, the man who carried Jesus' cross

WHAT DOES THE BIBLE SAY?

1 What does Exodus 9:16 tell you about God's primary purpose?

2 Where did Jesus get his sense of purpose from? Look at Matthew 26:42, 53–54, 56; John 3:14–15; 12:27–28.

3 How central was Christ's death to God's plan and purpose? Read Ephesians 3:10–12 and 2 Timothy 1:8–10. How does this affect your understanding of the cross?

4 What encouragement and challenges does Isaiah 55:11 give us regarding the purposes of God's word?

5 Psalm 33:11 says, 'The plans of the Lord stand firm forever, the purposes of his heart through all generations' (cf. Proverbs 19:21; Isaiah 46:10). If God will achieve his purposes no matter what, then what value is our obedience and what difference do our prayers make?

6 Look at Philippians 2:12–13 below – how will God's purposes be worked out in our lives? What is God's role and what is our

role? In what ways do you think God works in us to achieve his purposes?

> [12]*Therefore, my dear friends, as you have always obeyed – not only in my presence, but now much more in my absence – continue to work out your salvation with fear and trembling, [13]for it is God who works in you to will and to act according to his good purpose.*

LIFE FOCUS

Simon, the man who carried Jesus' cross: *'Almost there. We're nearly there. Almost done.'*

- In Philippians 2:2 Paul talks about his desire that believers would be 'like-minded'. What actions and attitudes need to be in place for there to be a unity of spirit and purpose in your church?

- What gives us a sense of purpose? Where should we start our search?

- What purpose or mission has Jesus given you? Considering your particular skills, gifts and interests, where do you think God wants you to serve him? Using the term 'ministry' in its widest sense, what ministry do you think God has designed and equipped you for?

- What is the value of knowing your purpose and God-given mission in life? For example, how does it help in decision-making and prioritising?

- What lessons can we learn from Jesus about how to maintain our focus? Are there priorities, pleasures or other legitimate activities you need to put aside in order to fulfil God's particular purpose for your life?

- What common fears and anxieties hold Christians back from following God's will for their life?

RESPONSE

In twos pray through some of the issues that have arisen from this week's study.

If you are able, be honest with your prayer partner and share:
- If you're not sure where/how God wants you to serve him
- If you have been ignoring God's will for your life and need to repent
- If you seem at a crossroads in God's will and need new direction
- If you know God's will for you but need his strength to obey

Discuss practical measures you can take and how the group can support you, then pray through these issues together.

Remember as you pray to God 'Not as I will, but as you will', Jesus prayed it before you (Matthew 26:39).

FURTHER STUDY

Rick Warren has written two very popular books on this topic – *Purpose Driven Life* and *Purpose Driven Church*.

THE STRUGGLE FOR POWER

Jesus: *'I am the good shepherd. I lay down my life for my sheep. No one takes my life from me but I lay it down of my own accord. I have power to lay it down and power to take it up again. This command is from my father.'*

THE BIG IDEA

There is a power play throughout the film as the Roman governor and Jewish authorities wrestle for control and public approval. In the face of this, Jesus' awareness of his own power and authority is surprising. The soldiers and religious leaders inflicted the cruellest punishment imaginable but he carried himself with a dignity that came from knowing he was allowing this to happen to him for God's sake and for ours. He didn't lose his life; he used his power to give it up willingly.

Ask yourself…

In what ways is God's power evident in your life? Are you relying on his power on a daily basis? Would you notice the difference in your marriage, family, work and church ministry if God removed his power?

TAKE 2

Pilate: *'I have the power the crucify you, or else set you free.'*

Jesus: *'You have no power over me except what is given you from above.'*

- How does the film portray the main characters using and abusing their power? Consider:
    - Jesus
    - Herod
    - Pilate
    - the religious leaders
    - the devil

WHAT DOES THE BIBLE SAY?

1 Psalm 150:2 says *'Praise him [God] for his acts of power; praise him for his surpassing greatness.'* In what ways has God demonstrated his power? Brainstorm as many ideas as you can.

2 Jesus didn't come with the military power that was expected of the Messiah. But in what other ways did he demonstrate power? See Luke 5:17, 9:1; 1 Corinthians 1:17; Colossians 2:15; Philippians 3:10; Hebrews 1:3.

3 What are the pitfalls of relying on our own human power? Look at 2 Chronicles 26:11–16; Ecclesiastes 4:1; Psalm 147:10–11.

4 Explain Paul's line of argument from 1 Corinthians 1:17–2:5 in your own words. What does he say the relationship between God's power and man's weakness is?

> *[17]For Christ did not send me to baptize, but to preach the gospel – not with words of human wisdom, lest the cross of Christ be emptied of its power.*

[18]*For the message of the cross is foolishness to those who are perishing, but to us who are being saved it is the power of God.* [19]*For it is written:*

'I will destroy the wisdom of the wise;
the intelligence of the intelligent I will frustrate.'

[20]*Where is the wise man? Where is the scholar? Where is the philosopher of this age? Has not God made foolish the wisdom of the world?* [21]*For since in the wisdom of God the world through its wisdom did not know him, God was pleased through the foolishness of what was preached to save those who believe.* [22]*Jews demand miraculous signs and Greeks look for wisdom,* [23]*but we preach Christ crucified: a stumbling block to Jews and foolishness to Gentiles,* [24]*but to those whom God has called, both Jews and Greeks, Christ the power of God and the wisdom of God.* [25]*For the foolishness of God is wiser than man's wisdom, and the weakness of God is stronger than man's strength.*

[26]*Brothers, think of what you were when you were called. Not many of you were wise by human standards; not many were influential; not many were of noble birth.* [27]*But God chose the foolish things of the world to shame the wise; God chose the weak things of the world to shame the strong.* [28]*He chose the lowly things of this world and the despised things – and the things that are not – to nullify the things that are,* [29]*so that no one may boast before him.* [30]*It is because of him that you are in Christ Jesus, who has become for us wisdom from God – that is, our righteousness, holiness and redemption.* [31]*Therefore, as it is written: 'Let him who boasts boast in the Lord.'*

[1]*When I came to you, brothers, I did not come with eloquence or superior wisdom as I proclaimed to you the testimony about God.* [2]*For I resolved to know nothing while I was with you except Jesus Christ and him crucified.* [3]*I came to you in weakness and fear, and with much trembling.* [4]*My message and my preaching were not with wise and persuasive words, but with a demonstration of the Spirit's power,* [5]*so that your faith might not rest on men's wisdom, but on God's power.*

5 Why do we need God's power? What difference does it make in our lives? Look at the following references to start your discussion:

- Romans 15:13
- Ephesians 3:16–19
- Colossians 1:10–11
- 2 Thessalonians 1:11
- 2 Timothy 1:8

LIFE FOCUS

Caiaphas, the High Priest: *'I ask you now Jesus of Nazareth, tell us, are you the Messiah, the son of the living God?'*

Jesus: *'I AM. And you will see the Son of Man seated at the right hand of power and coming on the clouds of heaven.'*

- When we appreciate the extent of God's power what should our proper response be?

- What factors stop us living and serving God in the full power of the Holy Spirit?

- In what ways have you seen God demonstrating his power through your weakness?

- How Christ-like are you in your exercise of power and authority? What lessons could you learn from Jesus? What practical changes would this involve in your particular context?

- Jesus used his power to liberate people from the power of Satan. Where are Satan's strongholds today – in what places or institutions is Satan having free reign? In what ways should Christians oppose or counter-balance Satan's power?

- In what sense is the church a powerful institution? How can we prevent it abusing this power?

RESPONSE

In twos pray through some of the issues that have arisen from this week's study.

Pray about:
- A Christ-like exercise of power in your home, workplace, church.
- Areas of your life you need to submit to God's power and authority.
- Ways to demonstrate God's power in Satan's territory.

Finish your session by praising God for the ways he has shown his power in your life and for his grace in giving us this power. If it is helpful, use the following Bible verses as a focus for your prayers:

'His divine power has given us everything we need for life and godliness through our knowledge of him who called us by his own glory and goodness. Through these he has given us his very great and precious promises, so that through them you may participate in the divine nature and escape the corruption in the world caused by evil desires.' 2 Peter 1:3–4.

'But we have this treasure in jars of clay to show that this all-surpassing power is from God and not from us.' 2 Corinthians 4:7

'I pray also that the eyes of your heart may be enlightened in order that you may know the hope to which he has called you, the riches of his glorious inheritance in the saints, and his incomparable power for us who believe. That power is like the working of his mighty strength, which he exerted in Christ when he raised him from the dead and seated him at his right hand in the heavenly realms.' Ephesians 1:18–19

FURTHER STUDY

When You Need a Miracle – by Lloyd John Ogilvie challenges us to remember the unlimited power of God on our behalf and looks at how men and women of the Bible experienced that power.

Selwyn Hughes has written about the work of the Holy Spirit and the role he wants to have in our lives in *The Holy Spirit – Our Counsellor*.

THE PROOF
OF LOVE

> Jesus: *'You've heard it said you shall love your neighbour and hate your enemy. But I say to you love your enemies and pray for those who persecute you. For if you only love those who love you what reward is there in that?'*

THE BIG IDEA

You would never call the film a love story, but in essence it is. It depicts every thread of love we're familiar with – a mother's love for her son, the love of friends for each other, the love of power and pleasure, even cruelty. But the most dramatic display of love was Jesus' love for us. His love was dramatic because it wasn't demonstrated in the usual way with kind words or a token gift. He demonstrated his love by obeying God's plan and going to the cross – by giving himself, by dying in our place for our sins. We say we love many things and we give our time, money and affections to many things. But Jesus' example challenges us to a higher standard of love: to love God and men with the same radical type of self-giving love he did.

Ask yourself…

What do you love most? What people, possessions, ideas, values and places do you love most?

TAKE 2

Jesus: *'There is no greater love than for a man to lay down his life for his friends.'*

- In the film there are many demonstrations of love but what particular example of love was most powerful for you? Consider what scene, moment or phrase had the most impact on you.

WHAT DOES THE BIBLE SAY?

1 How could the cruelty and horror of the cross ever be considered proof of God's love for us? Be specific, what do the following verses reveal to us about how the cross demonstrates God's love – John 3:16; Romans 5:8; 1 John 4:9–10?

2 How was love demonstrated in the early church community? Look at Acts 2:42–47; Romans 15:25–27; 1 Peter 4:8.

3 1 Corinthians 13:4–7 are probably the Bible's most well known verses on love. Look at the verses immediately before and after this passage. How does the context help you understand the meaning and implication of these verses?

4 How can our love for Jesus be demonstrated in the way we love our spouse and children? How can we translate Ephesians 5:22–6:4 (below) into practice? Give specific examples of how Christ's love can be seen in our homes and family relationships.

> *²²Wives, submit to your husbands as to the Lord. ²³For the husband is the head of the wife as Christ is the head of the church, his body, of which he is the Savior. ²⁴Now as the church submits to Christ, so also wives should submit to their husbands in everything.*

²⁵Husbands, love your wives, just as Christ loved the church and gave himself up for her ²⁶to make her holy, cleansing her by the washing with water through the word, ²⁷and to present her to himself as a radiant church, without stain or wrinkle or any other blemish, but holy and blameless. ²⁸In this same way, husbands ought to love their wives as their own bodies. He who loves his wife loves himself. ²⁹After all, no one ever hated his own body, but he feeds and cares for it, just as Christ does the church – ³⁰for we are members of his body. ³¹'For this reason a man will leave his father and mother and be united to his wife, and the two will become one flesh.' ³²This is a profound mystery – but I am talking about Christ and the church. ³³However, each one of you also must love his wife as he loves himself, and the wife must respect her husband.

¹Children, obey your parents in the Lord, for this is right. ²'Honor your father and mother' – which is the first commandment with a promise – ³'that it may go well with you and that you may enjoy long life on the earth.' ⁴Fathers, do not exasperate your children; instead, bring them up in the training and instruction of the Lord.

5 How do we grow in love? How do we increase in our love for others? Look at Galatians 5:22–23 and 2 Peter 1:5–8 for some ideas.

LIFE FOCUS

Jesus: 'I cannot be with you much longer, my friends. You cannot go where I am going. My commandment to you after I am gone is this … Love one another. As I have loved you, so love one another.'

- Jesus' commandment was *'As I have loved you, so love one another.'* What would Jesus' kind of love look like in your church community? Give specific practical examples.

- Why do we fail to love others in the church like Christ loves us? Discuss the following suggestions and other ideas of your own:
  - No sense of community
  - The fear of being hurt
  - The pressure of other commitments and preoccupations

- What would you say to a Christian friend who confides to you that they no longer feel God's love? They have lost the feelings they had when they first became a Christian – God used to speak so directly but now he doesn't seem to speak at all. They used to have lots of positive answers to prayer and now they are unsure whether God hears them anymore. God feels distant; they no longer feel the warmth of his presence and wonder if he still loves them.

- Paul reports to Timothy that their friend Demas was, *'in love with this present world'* (2 Timothy 4:10). In what ways are you tempted to love *'this present world'* too much? What are the warning signs that you are losing your love for God?

- Society encourages us to 'love yourself', to have 'me time', to 'love the skin you're in'. How do these messages compare/contrast with the Christian perspective on love? Are there any lessons we should learn from society about loving ourselves? What can Christians teach contemporary society about love? What are the best methods of getting our message across?

RESPONSE

In twos pray through some of the issues that have arisen from this week's study.

In particular consider Jesus' command to his followers: *'"Love the Lord your God with all your heart and with all your soul and with all your mind. " This is the first and greatest commandment. And the second is like it: "Love your neighbour as yourself." All the Law and Prophets hang on these two commandments.'* (Matthew 22:37–40)

Is it obvious God is your first love by the way you:
– spend your money
– prioritise your time
– care for others
– commit to the church community
– use your gifts
– serve in ministry
– treat your family

Discuss and pray through the changes you need to make so that your life reflects the love you have for God.

Close your session together by telling God why you love him. If it helps, use Psalm 136 as a model for your prayers and praises. As a group write your own version of this Psalm praising God for specific ways he has acted on your behalf.

¹Give thanks to the LORD, for he is good.
His love endures forever.
²Give thanks to the God of gods.
His love endures forever.
³Give thanks to the Lord of lords:
His love endures forever.

⁴to him who alone does great wonders,
His love endures forever.
⁵who by his understanding made the heavens,
His love endures forever.

⁶who spread out the earth upon the waters,
His love endures forever.

⁷who made the great lights
His love endures forever.
⁸the sun to govern the day,
His love endures forever.
⁹the moon and stars to govern the night;
His love endures forever.

¹⁰to him who struck down the firstborn of Egypt
His love endures forever.
¹¹and brought Israel out from among them
His love endures forever.
¹²with a mighty hand and outstretched arm;
His love endures forever.

¹³to him who divided the Red Sea asunder
His love endures forever.
¹⁴and brought Israel through the midst of it,
His love endures forever.
¹⁵but swept Pharaoh and his army into the Red Sea;
His love endures forever.

¹⁶ to him who led his people through the desert,
His love endures forever.
¹⁷who struck down great kings,
His love endures forever.
¹⁸and killed mighty kings
His love endures forever.

¹⁹Sihon king of the Amorites
His love endures forever.
²⁰and Og king of Bashan
His love endures forever.
²¹and gave their land as an inheritance,
His love endures forever.
²²an inheritance to his servant Israel;
His love endures forever.

²³*to the One who remembered us in our low estate*
His love endures forever.
²⁴*and freed us from our enemies,*
His love endures forever.
²⁵*and who gives food to every creature.*
His love endures forever.

²⁶*Give thanks to the God of heaven.*
His love endures forever.

FURTHER STUDY

In *The Difficult Doctrine of the Love of God*, D.A. Carson introduces us to the vast theme of God's love. He addresses the difficult issue of how God's justice, wrath, and sovereignty are compatible with his love and so seeks to give us a more truthful perspective on this inexhaustible subject.

THE COST OF DISCIPLESHIP

A religious leader to the Roman governor: *'So far the High Priest hasn't told you this man's greatest crime. He has become the leader of a large and dangerous sect who hail him as the Son of David! He claims that he is the Messiah, the king promised to the Jews ...'*

THE BIG IDEA

Three years. One would have thought that three years would have been time enough to train his twelve disciples into an effective team. But they still didn't understand his teaching, didn't anticipate his death or resurrection, and at the first sign of trouble they fled the Garden of Gethsemane. Judas betrayed him and Peter denied him. Yet we don't judge these men because we recognise ourselves in them – good intentions marred by weakness, fear and greed. We share the same sense of failure, the misunderstandings and disappointment in ourselves. But the film also gives us hope that true discipleship is possible. Perhaps the most graphic picture of discipleship is Simon, a passer-by, who ended up carrying a cross which wasn't his. At first he was reluctant; he had his own plans to be busy with. But eventually he shared the burden of the cross and cared for the wounded Saviour and, as he did so, identified himself with Jesus. Despite our many failures that is the kind of discipleship Jesus longs for from us.

Ask yourself...

What message would you have trusted these twelve men with? Why did Jesus trust them?

TAKE 2

Peter: *'Wherever you go, Lord, I will follow. To prison, even to death.'*

Jesus: *'Amen, I say to you before the cock crows you will deny me three times.'*

- How did the film portray discipleship? Think about how it demonstrated both true discipleship and failure? Consider the actions, emotions and speech of:
    - Judas
    - Peter
    - Mary
    - Simon, the man who carried Jesus' cross
    - John
    - the disciples in Gethsemane

WHAT DOES THE BIBLE SAY?

1 Read Luke 14:25–33 below. What point was Jesus trying to make in these verses? What did he mean when he said that his disciples must 'hate' their family members and 'carry their cross'? Paraphrase these verses in your own words in order to come up with a contemporary job description for a disciple.

> *[25]Large crowds were traveling with Jesus, and turning to them he said: [26]'If anyone comes to me and does not hate his father and mother, his wife and children, his brothers and sisters – yes, even his own life – he cannot be my disciple. [27]And anyone who does not carry his cross and follow me cannot be my disciple.'*

> *[28]'Suppose one of you wants to build a tower. Will he not first sit down and estimate the cost to see if he has enough money to complete it? [29]For if he lays the foundation and is not able to*

finish it, everyone who sees it will ridicule him, [30]saying, "This fellow began to build and was not able to finish."'

[31]'Or suppose a king is about to go to war against another king. Will he not first sit down and consider whether he is able with ten thousand men to oppose the one coming against him with twenty thousand? [32]If he is not able, he will send a delegation while the other is still a long way off and will ask for terms of peace. [33]In the same way, any of you who does not give up everything he has cannot be my disciple.'

2 What can we learn from 1 Corinthians 9:24–27 and Hebrews 12:1–3 about the type of discipline involved in being a disciple? What kind of practices and habits were the writers advocating?

3 As disciples of Jesus how should we expect to be treated by the world? What scenarios does the Bible depict? Look at John 15:18–21 and 1 Corinthians 4:9–16 for example.

4 Look at John 21:20–22. What do you learn about discipleship from these verses?

5 What are the rewards of discipleship? For some ideas look at Mark 10:28–31, 2 Timothy 4:6–8, Revelation 2:26–27.

LIFE FOCUS

Soldier: *'You! Yes, you! Get over here!'*

Passer-by: *'What do you want from me?'*

Soldier: *'This criminal can't carry his cross by himself anymore. You will help him! Now get going!'*

Passer-by: *'I can't do that. It's none of my business. Get someone else!'*

Soldier: *'Do as I tell you. Now move! Let's go!'*

Passer-by: *'All right, but remember I'm an innocent man, forced to carry the cross of a condemned man.'*

- Matthew records Jesus' last words to his followers, *'Go and make disciples of all nations, baptising them in the name of the Father and of the Son and of the Holy Spirit, and teaching them to obey everything I have commanded you.'* In our context how do we help people become disciples and not just converts? What programmes, strategies, relationships, practices etc. do we need to put in place?

- Jesus didn't teach his disciples in a classroom but in fields, by the sea, in the synagogue, in people's homes – wherever he was ministering. What places, occasions, people and circumstances has God used to teach you and make you a more mature disciple?

- Consider Jesus' method of discipleship training: he hand-picked twelve men and for three years they lived life together. Is Jesus' model of training an appropriate one for today? How could it work practically in your church? How would you adapt it? What would be the objections raised and how would you answer them?

- 'Mentoring' and 'imitating' are currently two key words associated with discipleship. What do they mean and how do they work out in practice? What are the positive advantages and dangers of mentoring and imitating?

- Where along the road of discipleship would you describe yourself?
    - Interested in the journey but not yet a disciple.
    - Just started out on the journey.
    - Been travelling a while but finding the terrain difficult at present.
    - A seasoned traveller but still discovering new places of interest to investigate.

RESPONSE

In twos pray through some of the issues that have arisen from this week's study.

If you are able, be honest with a prayer partner and share what God has taught you from this study:

- Are you like Simon saying to God, 'It's none of my business. Get someone else'? Will you put your own agenda and legitimate concerns aside to carry Christ's cross?

- Are you a flabby disciple, lacking spiritual muscle? What disciplines, spiritual habits and practices will you make part of your daily routine?

- Do you need to bring your focus back to Christ and stop comparing how God is treating you with how he is treating other people?

- If life is difficult at the moment will you concentrate on the rewards of discipleship which will be yours one day?

- Will you consider your present circumstances, the problems as well as the pleasures, and ask God what he wants you to learn? What in your life is God using to make you a more mature disciple?

- Who are you learning from? Who is your role model? Is there an older Christian you could spend time with, pray with and receive spiritual counsel?

Decide what God is saying to you and how you will respond. If it helps to make your commitment more concrete you could write it down on a piece of paper and keep it in your Bible as a reminder to yourself.

Close your session together by discussing as a group how you can help each other become more effective disciples.

FURTHER STUDY

John Ortberg has written two very practical books on discipleship – *The Life You've Always Wanted* and *If You Want to Walk on Water You've Got to Get Out of The Boat*.

LEADER'S GUIDE

You need to plan the timings of each session and decide which questions you will concentrate on.

Aim to tackle all the questions under WHAT DOES THE BIBLE SAY? and choose a couple more from the LIFE FOCUS section. Select the ones most relevant to the needs and interests of your particular group. Leave enough time for the RESPONSE section so that every member of the group can focus on how they personally need to respond to what God has been saying to them through the study.

Have tapes/CDs and music systems ready to use in the RESPONSE section.

Encourage people to prepare their answers to the questions in advance so they are ready to discuss the issues.

Remind people to bring a Bible with them so that you can look up the Scripture references together. It is important to read the Bible verses you are studying together during the session. Where Scripture references are quoted in full, the NIV translation has been used. However, it may also be helpful to use a variety of Bible translations in your study so that you can understand and get an accurate sense of the meaning of particular verses.

Remember not everyone will have seen the film or recollect every scene of it so allow people to discuss the film in the TAKE 2 section but do not spend too long on this section. If you have time you could review certain sections of the film together.

At the end of the book there are some suggestions to help you lead each study. A list of materials for each section is given as well as suggested answers for the WHAT DOES THE BIBLE SAY? sections. No answers are given for the LIFE FOCUS part of the study as these questions are intended for people to reflect on their own ideas and relate biblical truths to their current life situations. There are no particular right answers so encourage the group to share and explain their views, listen to each other, and try to come to a consensus if possible.

THE STRUCTURE OF EACH SESSION

THE BIG IDEA

This summary statement is to help set the scene, focus on the theme for the study and remind you how this particular issue was dealt with in the film. You can read this summary paragraph to the group or encourage them to read it before you meet together.

TAKE 2

Use this opening section as an icebreaker, encouraging people to talk about the film and the issues it raises. You might like to watch certain parts of the film again to highlight particular themes or to refresh people's memories.

WHAT DOES THE BIBLE SAY?

These questions give you the opportunity to look at the theme from a biblical perspective. Encourage people to look up the Scripture verses and answer the questions in their own words whilst being as specific as possible.

LIFE FOCUS

Use this section as an opportunity to allow the group to share their views, experiences, and backgrounds. Encourage people to see how the Bible passages they have just looked at can relate to everyday life situations.

RESPONSE

The study guide gives a suggestion as to how you might like to wrap your session up. But be flexible and be willing to allow people to respond to what God has been saying to them in an appropriate way. You may like to have CDs/tapes and a music system available so that you can sing or listen to songs as part of this time.

FURTHER STUDY

For each session, books are suggested so that individuals can study the issues further.

SESSION ONE

NOTES

MATERIALS

- A TV and video/DVD of *The Passion of the Christ* if you would like to review sections of the film.
- Bibles.
- A flip chart to record people's answers.
- Pens and paper for question 4.
- CDs/tapes and a music system for the RESPONSE section.

WHAT DOES THE BIBLE SAY?

1. **John** tells us that Jesus' truth was about God's kingdom and how one could become part of that. Jesus explained that entry – salvation – was through cleansing from sin and the Holy Spirit's work in one's life **(3:3, 5)**. He explained further that this salvation, this eternal life, could be accessed by hearing God's word and believing in him **(5:24)**. Jesus' truth was also concerned with who he was. He explained he was the bread from heaven, like the manna in the desert, which can nourish and sustain people **(6:32)**, he is also eternal and divine **(8:58)**. Jesus' truth focused on his relationship to his father which was one of dependence and submission **(5:19)**. So essentially Jesus' truth centred around the contents of the gospel and his role in the world.

2. It is inherent in Jesus' character to be truthful. He himself is true, therefore he is the yardstick by which we can measure everything and everyone else. He is completely trustworthy and

what he says he will do, he will keep his promises. His judgements, his words, his decisions and actions can be relied upon to be full of integrity, honesty and righteousness.

3. **John 17:17** – God's aim is to make us holy through his word. As we read the Bible, God's truth challenges and purifies us, making us more like Jesus. **Psalm 96:13** – Because God is truth he is qualified to judge the world rightly. **Job 37:16** – God's knowledge is perfect, i.e. it is true therefore his activity in the world and his decisions are always based on a true understanding and perception of the world.

4. Perhaps give people time to paraphrase the verses if they have not prepared, then invite them to share their ideas with the group. The general ideas behind these verses are as follows: **Exodus 20:16** – God expects us to be truthful, not to lie to or about others. **Psalm 51:6** – God expects moral integrity. **John 4:23–24** – God expects our worship to be based on the truth of who he is and what he has revealed about himself in his living and written word, Jesus and the Scriptures. **John 16:13** – we are to allow ourselves to be guided by the Holy Spirit, the spirit of truth. **Ephesians 4:15** – we are to speak the truth lovingly to other Christians so that together as a community we can grow to Christian maturity.

5. The freedom we have as Christians comes when we obey and live out Jesus' teachings. This freedom is not a licence to do as we please but it is freedom from sin's hold over us. Without Christ, everyone is a slave to sin because they cannot stop themselves sinning. But through his death Jesus broke the power of sin and if we trust in him he will release us from that power so that we are free to live the life God wants for us, free to serve him.

SESSION TWO

NOTES

MATERIALS

- A TV and video/DVD of *The Passion of the Christ* if you would like to review sections of the film.
- Bibles.
- A flip chart to record people's answers.
- CDs/tapes and a music system for the RESPONSE section.

WHAT DOES THE BIBLE SAY?

1. **Job** indicates that although Satan perpetrated the suffering it was allowed by God. God was aware of Satan's plans, gave his permission and set the boundaries for what he could do. **Isaiah** and **Amos** say that God creates disasters, most probably referring to what we would term 'natural disasters', like the plagues in Egypt for example. In **2 Corinthians** Paul refers to his affliction as a 'messenger of Satan', again suggesting that Satan perpetrated his suffering, but he prayed to God because he was the one who had the power to remove it. All the references seem to indicate that ultimately God knows and has the power over suffering but he gives Satan freedom to inflict pain and hardship. On the one hand, it is comforting to know that God is sovereign and in control; on the other hand, it is difficult to understand why he does not stop our pain – answering the other questions may help you deal with this issue rather than fully discussing it here.

2. **Galatians** – suffering can be a result of our own sinfulness. **Hebrews** – suffering can be God's discipline because he loves

us and wants to make us more holy. **1 Peter** – suffering can purify our faith and to prove it is genuine. Our godly response to suffering brings God glory. **Psalm 119** – suffering can keep us focused on God and obedient to him, perhaps because in affliction we need to depend on him more fully. **Job** – suffering helps us gain a bigger perspective of what God is doing in the world. We realise we can't always understand his ways or his reasoning and we have to leave our questions about suffering to him.

3. Moses had to deal with the constant criticism of the Israelites and the burden of having to look after them in the desert. Jeremiah felt let down by God because of the response he received as a prophet. He was made fun of, insulted and mocked by Judah. He had the dilemma of wanting to keep God's word to himself to protect his reputation but at the same time felt the compunction to speak out. Even his friends waited for him to make a mistake. In Corinthians Paul recalls the catalogue of physical suffering he endured as an apostle, the occasions he faced danger, lacked basic necessities, and the overwhelming pressure of his care and concern for the churches. John was exiled to the island of Patmos because of his beliefs. These men demonstrate that suffering of all kinds is to be expected in the service of Christ, even when you are serving his people! We can learn from the honest assessment of their suffering, the way they talked openly to God about it and even blamed him at times. Most importantly as leaders they brought their complaints to God and let him avenge the wrong done to them and act on their behalf. John talks of 'patient endurance' and Paul refers to protecting the ministry and the great rewards of following God – clearly both of these men had no regrets about their life of service.

4. **Psalm 22** – he was forsaken by God **(v1)**; he was despised, rejected and mocked by men **(v6-8)**; his bones were out of joint, strength evaporated, he was thirsty **(v14-15)**; his hands and feet were pierced and the soldiers cast lots for his clothes **(v16-18)**.

Zechariah 11:12 – thirty pieces of silver could be a reference to the price Judas received for betraying Jesus; **13:7** Jesus is the Good Shepherd who was killed and his sheep, the apostles, fled with fear. **Isaiah 52:13–53:12** – he was raised from the dead **(v13)**; the torture disfigured him **(v14)**; he came from humble roots and was not particularly physically attractive **(v2)**; he was despised and rejected by his contemporaries and knew suffering well **(v3)**; we thought he was suffering on the cross for his own sins but really he was suffering for ours **(v4)**; his hands and feet were pierced for our salvation **(v5)**; he did not reply to the religious and political leaders who questioned him, he did not argue with them or try to defend himself **(v7)**; his death earned him a grave among the criminals but Joseph of Arimathea, a rich man, gave him his tomb **(v9)**. Invite the group to share their thoughts on the fact that God planned Jesus' death and suffering in advance. What does this indicate about God's plans and what he thinks of us?

5. **Matthew** says making Jesus a priority and taking up his lifestyle of cross-carrying will mean self-denial, letting go of our agenda and plans and following his. It also means that family commitments need to take a lesser place. **Acts** says the apostles suffered for Jesus' name, they suffered for being associated with him and for upholding his values. **1 Peter** indicates we can suffer because we have done wrong but the Christian will suffer for righteousness that the State or society does not appreciate. So the 'sufferings of Christ' seem to be any type of suffering which is a consequence of our being associated with Christ and living out his values. It will mean sharing the mockery, insults and pain that Christ did on the cross.

SESSION THREE

NOTES

MATERIALS

- A TV and video/DVD of *The Passion of the Christ* if you would like to review sections of the film.
- Bibles.
- A flip chart to record people's answers.
- CDs/tapes and a music system for the RESPONSE section.

WHAT DOES THE BIBLE SAY?

1. **Hebrews 9:22** explains God's law that blood was needed for the forgiveness of sins (atonement), the principle was a life for a life – the life of the sacrifice took the place of the one being forgiven. **Hebrews 9:13–14, 25–28** explain that the blood of animals could only bring outward cleansing; it could not cleanse our consciences. These sacrifices were inadequate; they were a temporary measure which had to be repeated annually. However, Jesus was unblemished **(v14)**, he was the only human who was pure and holy. Therefore he was the only one who could do God's will and act as a substitute for us, dying for our sins and not his own, cleansing us fully from sin by his once-and-for-all death on the cross.

2. **Acts 10:43** – we need to believe in Jesus, this implies not just a belief that he exists but a trust in him and personal commitment of ourselves to him. **Acts 20:21** – we need to repent and have faith in God. This means a turning away from sin and a lifestyle alienated from God and a turning to him, trusting him for our present and future and relying on his strength to live his way.

Luke 6:37 – we must forgive others. God gives us the strength to make these decisions and to keep them **(Eph. 2:8)** but there must be an element of our willingness because God seeks disciples who want to love and follow him not just conform to his standards out of duty **(Deut. 6:5)**. He wants a living relationship with his people not robots. We must forgive because it reflects the transformation Christ's forgiveness has made in our lives, it shows the reality of our faith and God's strength in us **(Eph. 4:32)**.

3. **Psalm 103:12** – our sins are separated from us as far as the East is from the West, a limitless distance. **Isaiah 38:17** – our sins are behind God's back, they are out of his sight. **Isaiah 43:25** – he rubs our sins out as if he took an eraser and removed them from the record book. **Micah 7:19** – he destroys and eradicates our sins by trampling them under his feet and dumping them into the sea. Encourage the group to come up with modern day analogies. For example God putting our sins in a landfill site.

4. In **Luke 23:39–43** we learn that Jesus was willing to forgive a thief as he was dying. Despite the man's evil life Jesus was willing to forgive him at this late stage. **Jonah 3:10; 4:1–3, 11** – the Ninevites were the cruellest nation of their day, they were enemies of the Israelites and yet when they repented of their sins God forgave them. As Jonah said, God is gracious and compassionate, infinitely patient waiting for people to repent. These verses and other examples the group can cite reveal God's great desire to forgive. God is eager to be our God and for us to be his people, and act like it.

5. The Bible references seem to indicate that our forgiveness of others is a result as well as a condition of God forgiving us. We forgive others because we have been forgiven by God and recognise our daily need for forgiveness. Our forgiveness is not based on the other person's repentance – how they respond should not affect our actions towards them.

SESSION FOUR

NOTES

MATERIALS

- A TV and video/DVD of *The Passion of the Christ* if you would like to review sections of the film.

- Bibles.

- A flip chart to record people's answers.

- CDs/tapes and a music system for the RESPONSE section.

WHAT DOES THE BIBLE SAY?

1. **Isaiah 14:12–15** could be a description of how Satan originated. He was an important heavenly being **(v12)**, an angel, who thought he could make himself equal to God in status and authority. His punishment was being cast out of heaven. **2 Peter 2:4** and **Jude 6** also explain that some angels did sin. They were proud and unwilling to accept their assigned place in heaven. So they were removed from their positions and from the presence of God in heaven. The verses indicate they were put under some kind of restraining influence until the final judgement but this does not rule out their continued activity in the world.

2. **John 8:44** – the devil is a murderer and a liar; he gets his way by deception and violence. **2 Corinthians 4:4** – the devil is 'the god of this age' who will blind people's eyes so that they cannot see the truth of the gospel. **Ephesians 2:2** – he is 'the ruler of the kingdom of the air', he is a spiritual being who works in people's souls not an earthbound human. **1 Peter 5:8** – like a roaring lion he moves with stealth and is intent on devouring

believers. **1 John 2:13** – he is called 'the evil one' and will use foul means against us. **Revelation 12:9, 10** – he is called 'the ancient serpent' referring to his role in history, beginning in the Garden of Eden. As in the garden he attempts, by subtle means, to lead us astray. He is also called the 'accuser' – whereas God forgives our sins and remembers them no more, the Devil constantly reminds us of the wrong we have done. He attempts to defeat us and wear us out by reminding us of our past sins.

3. **2 Corinthians 2:5–11** – we need to use church discipline to lovingly restore individuals, we need to forgive them and incorporate them back into the fellowship because if we don't Satan will have his way through disunity and bitterness. **2 Corinthians 11:12–15** – unbelievers with a hidden agenda may come into the church, take positions of leadership and become influential, without us realising it. **2 Timothy 2:24–26** – the devil may influence people to oppose God's leaders and biblical teaching and blind them so that they cannot recognise the truth. **Revelation 2:10** – Satan may inflict persecution and even death on believers.

4. Discuss what it means in daily life to 'put on' truth, righteousness, readiness, faith, salvation and the word of God? How do we put on these attributes; how do we demonstrate them in our work and home life? What does it mean to pray in the Spirit? Perhaps some ways of putting on the armour of God would be to have a time with God reading the Bible and praying before your day begins, spending time with him and his people, daily repentance, telling the truth at work on your expense claims and taxes, and making righteous decisions even when they don't bring the company profits for example.

5. **Malachi** reminds us that although the evil prosper now and we may wonder what the point of serving God is, God knows who are his and one day the distinction between the godly and ungodly will be plain for all to see. The wicked will face judgement and it will be inflicted on them by the righteous. The righteous, however, will be renewed, their salvation complete.

SESSION FIVE

NOTES

MATERIALS

- A TV and video/DVD of *The Passion of the Christ* if you would like to review sections of the film.

- Bibles.

- A flip chart to record people's answers.

- CDs/tapes and a music system for the RESPONSE section.

WHAT DOES THE BIBLE SAY?

1. God's purpose is to show his power to, in and through people. He wants the whole world to know and honour him. Essentially he wants his glory to be acknowledged universally and people to respond.

2. **Matthew 26:42** tells us that Jesus derived his sense of purpose from doing God's will. Doing what God wanted gave him focus, direction and a sense of purpose. **Matthew 26:53–54, 56** indicates Jesus gained purpose from knowing that he was fulfilling a plan, he was fulfilling ancient prophecies pointing to his unmistakable divinity. **John 3:14–15** tells us that Jesus derived purpose from knowing his death would grant eternal life to others, he knew there was eternal significance to his suffering. **John 12:27–28** says Jesus' purpose was to bring God glory.

3. **Ephesians 3:10–12** tells us that Christ's death was God's eternal intention, his plan before the beginning of time. **2 Timothy 1:8–10** also says Christ's death was central to God's plan to bring us salvation, it was his purpose, it was agreed before the beginning of time, it was his way of securing eternal life for us, it

was the crux of the good news he offers. These verses remind us that the cross was not a mistake when evil men triumphed but God's eternal rescue plan because he loved us so much. That God was willing for his own son to endure such cruelty would indicate that salvation could not be accomplished by any other means.

4. **Isaiah** reminds us that God's word will always accomplish his will. God's word in this chapter refers particularly to repentance – God's word will work in individuals' hearts and draw them to salvation. We can be encouraged that God's word is sufficient to do this, it is his responsibility, he will save those he wills. The challenge is: are we proclaiming, teaching, sharing God's word? Are we letting it loose so that it can have the desired effect? We need not worry who it is God will save, only whether we are playing our part in making his word known.

5. God will accomplish his purposes by whatever means he chooses. However, he gives us the honour of joining him and being part of his plans. We do not work to make something happen that would otherwise not have happened. Rather we are obedient to bring God glory; we pray to align our will to his. Our obedience and prayers bring pleasure to God and please his heart because they show our desire to conform to his will. We have the choice whether to be part of God's plans or to miss out on what he is doing in the world.

6. **Philippians 2:12–13** explains our role and God's role in our spiritual growth. God promises to work in us and through us to achieve his will in our lives and to make us more like Christ. But it is our responsibility to be involved and to work hard at that spiritual growth and development. For example, God promises to develop the fruit of the spirit in our lives but it is our responsibility to put ourselves in places and make associations that will aid that growth, such as being an active member of a local church, taking opportunities to use our spiritual gifts, relying on God's power in daily life etc.

SESSION SIX

NOTES

MATERIALS

- A TV and video/DVD of *The Passion of the Christ* if you would like to review sections of the film.

- Bibles.

- A flip chart to record people's answers.

- CDs/tapes and a music system for the RESPONSE section.

WHAT DOES THE BIBLE SAY?

1. Invite the group to come up with as many suggestions as they can. The following list is just a starting point. God has shown his power through creation; in our salvation; Jesus' resurrection; in the lives of his people, for example rescuing the Israelites from Egypt; through weak leaders such as Moses and David; through miracles like parting the Red Sea and sending manna.

2. **Luke 5:17** says Jesus showed his power through his healing ministry which he passed on to his apostles **(9:1)**. **1 Corinthians 1:17, Colossians 2:15** – Unlikely as it seemed at the time, the cross was a demonstration of Jesus' power over sin and all powers and authorities which stood opposed to him. **Philippians 3:10** – Jesus' resurrection was also proof of his power. **Hebrews 1:3** teaches that Jesus' powerful word holds everything that has been created together, his power sustains the universe.

3. The example of Uzziah in **2 Chronicles 26:11–16** warns us that when we grow powerful in worldly terms there is a tendency to

become proud, to disregard God and become less wholehearted in our devotion to him. Uzziah's worldly power meant he forgot his position in relation to God and took liberties; he entered the temple and took the role of a priest. **Ecclesiastes 4:1** warns how the powerful often abuse their might and use it to oppress others. **Psalm 147:10–11** reminds us that we can't impress God with our power and strength, we can't rely on it when God really wants our devotion.

4. Paul explains that the cross appears foolish but it is actually the power that saves men and women from sin. We look for worldly wisdom and miraculous signs but God has chosen the cross and the gospel to be the way of salvation. Only those whose hearts God has opened recognise his power and wisdom and realise that he is more powerful and wise than man's best efforts. In the same way, God's master-plan was to choose weak men and women to be his servants so that it was obvious the power they demonstrated was his. Paul explained that his own weakness, fear and lack of eloquence showcased the Holy Spirit's power working in him and convinced people that they were trusting in God's power not man's limited wisdom.

5. **Romans 15:13** – God's power gives us hope. **Ephesians 3:16–19** – we need God's power so that our lives may be right before him and he'd feel at home living within us. His power helps us understand and experience Christ's love and to grow to spiritual maturity. **Colossians 1:10–11** – we need God's power to patiently endure all the trials of life. **2 Thessalonians 1:11** – God's power is needed to achieve and complete all the good intentions God puts into our minds to do for him. **2 Timothy 1:8** – we need God's power to persevere and suffer for the gospel.

SESSION SEVEN

NOTES

MATERIALS

- A TV and video/DVD of *The Passion of the Christ* if you would like to review sections of the film.
- Bibles.
- A flip chart to record people's answers.
- Pens and paper for the RESPONSE section.
- CDs/tapes and a music system for the RESPONSE section.

WHAT DOES THE BIBLE SAY?

1. **John 3:16** tells how much God loves us because it stresses that he gave his only son to die and also that he wanted us to have eternal life. He wanted us to live forever with him rather than to perish. **Romans 5:8** reminds us that God loved us so much that he sent Jesus to die for us while we were still sinners – although we still rejected God and were hateful towards him he took the initiative to rescue us. **1 John 4:9–10** reiterates the thoughts expressed in the previous verses. God sent his only son into a sinful world where we did not love him, knowing that he would be crucified. His son was the salvation plan; there was no other way to fulfil the law's requirements for sin.

2. Love was demonstrated in the early church by their sense of community. **Acts 2:42–47** emphasises that the first Christians did not just devote themselves to teaching, prayer and worshipping God but they devoted themselves to each other. They shared each others' lives – this meant meeting each others'

needs and gathering together daily. Their worship of God was done communally and expressed itself in the way the community looked after each other and incorporated new members. **Romans 15:25–27** indicates love was shown by financial giving to believers in need. In particular Gentiles were giving to Jews – God's love crossed traditional barriers. In **1 Peter 4:8** love is demonstrated by overlooking the sins of other believers. This doesn't refer to sins which need to be addressed by the community. Rather it refers to overlooking the hurt we cause each other in the course of living together in order to heal and restore the bonds of fellowship. The verse means love does not hold on to grievances or petty squabbles but forgives again and again.

3. This passage on love is not referring to how to relate to your marriage partner, although it could equally apply here. The passage was written in the context of church worship and how to exercise our spiritual gifts. Perhaps this underlines how much love needs to be exercised within the church community. We often think of how to show love to unbelievers but effort needs to be given to loving those within the church. There will be conflicts and different view points particularly concerning how we worship but love is to be the overall focus. Our spiritual gifts are worthless if they are not exercised in love.

4. Encourage the group to come up with some practical suggestions. What does it mean for a husband to love his wife as Christ loved the church? It means a selfless and sacrificial love. The husband is to have a sanctifying influence on his wife; through his encouragement and example she should become more like Christ. For example, perhaps a husband could look after the children so his wife could have a quiet time or get out to a Bible study group. Perhaps he could initiate praying together. What does it mean for a husband to love his wife as he loves his own body? This self love probably means that a husband knows and cares for his wife's physical and emotional needs as he does his own. Paul doesn't ask the wives to love

their husbands but one can infer that the intelligent and willing submission (not doormat mentality) that he calls for is an expression of love. In practice perhaps this means not always trying to change your husband but showing him respect. Love for our children is seen in our care for them. The phrase 'bring them up' literally means to nourish and feed them. So we are to make sure they are feeding on God's word, making church accessible and familiar to them, teaching them God's truth etc. We are also to 'train them'. This refers to discipline and means setting and sticking to boundaries. Children's love for their parents is shown by obeying and honouring them.

5. There seems to be at least two elements to growing in love. On the one hand, love is a fruit of the spirit which will increase in our lives the more we spend time with God, read his word, pray, and become more like Christ. Love will be the result of a God-focused life **(Galatians 5:22–23)**. On the other hand, love is something we need to make a determined effort with; it is a conscious choice; an act of our will **(2 Peter 1:5–8)**.

SESSION EIGHT

NOTES

MATERIALS

- A TV and video/DVD of *The Passion of the Christ* if you would like to review sections of the film.
- Bibles.
- A flip chart to record people's answers.
- Pens and paper for question one and the RESPONSE section.
- CDs/tapes and a music system for the RESPONSE section.

WHAT DOES THE BIBLE SAY?

1. In **Luke 14:25–33** Jesus explains the cost of being his disciple. He uses hyperbole to stress that he must take priority over one's family; we must love and seek to please him more than we do our 'nearest and dearest'. Another requirement of discipleship is that we 'carry our cross' – this symbol of death portrays a denial of self and our own agenda and a willingness to be totally committed to Christ, willing to suffer, even die for his sake. The examples of estimating the cost before building a tower or going to war are to highlight that we must count the cost of commitment before we profess our allegiance to Jesus. He does not want naïve followers interested only in the benefits of Christianity. Followers of Christ must be willing to give up everything to serve him. Encourage members of the group to come up with their own paraphrases of these verses.

2. In **1 Corinthians 9:24–27** Paul talks of the prize God has for us in heaven. To receive that prize we need to maintain our focus;

instead of running the Christian life aimlessly we need to be rigorous in disciplining our bodies. Our bodies can be used either to serve God or to give in to sin and temptation. Practical examples of what Paul is referring to could be fasting, waking up early to have time with God, resisting excess of food, using our bodies to serve others rather than ourselves. **Hebrews 12:1–3** refers to removing everything that hinders us from running the Christian race effectively. For example, it is right to want to spend time with one's family but if that prevents you going where God calls you and obeying him then these ties need to be relegated and God given priority. We are told to run the race marked out for us, that is our individual race; we are not to look at the race other Christians are running and we should not compare ourselves to them. We are to keep Jesus as our focus and inspiration. Making sure we spend time alone with God, reading the Bible, and praying and worshipping him will help in this regard.

3. **John 15:18–21** indicates being hated by the world is only to be expected. If we believe and stand for the same things that Jesus did we can only expect that the world will react to us as it did to him. Persecution is inevitable. If we do not feel hated by the world perhaps we need to ask why. Is it because we are fitting in too well? In **1 Corinthians 4:9–16** Paul relates his own experience – he has been made a spectacle of, he compares himself to the man at the end of the procession on his way to die in the arena. He has been made a fool of for Christ's sake. He has been dishonoured; he is weak, hungry, and thirsty; he has been brutally treated, is homeless etc. He sums it all up by saying he has become the 'scum of the earth'. For most of us this is contrary to our experience and to what we strive for. Perhaps we need to adjust our expectations of what a 'successful' Christian looks like.

4. Peter was concerned about what Jesus would require of John, and Jesus' reply was 'What is that to you?' It is tempting to look at how God is treating other Christians, to look at what they are

giving up to follow him, and to base our decisions on that. As long as we seem to be better Christians that those around us we feel pleased with ourselves. These verses remind us that our journey of discipleship is between us and God – he may ask us to do things for him he has not asked anyone else in our generation. We are to be obedient and imitate Christ – no one else.

5. In **Mark 10:28–31** Jesus promises blessings and persecution in this life. We will receive back what we have given up for Christ but it will be in different forms. For example, if we have given up family for Christ's sake it will be made up to us by the relationships and fellowship we receive in the church body. In heaven we will also receive eternal life. Although God judges rewards differently to us he is no man's debtor, we can never out-give God. **2 Timothy 4:6–8** says that those who have remained faithful to God will receive a crown of righteousness in heaven. We don't know exactly what this crown will look like or what it represents but it is a reward for faithful service. **Revelation 2:26–27** tells us our reward will be authority to rule the nations, exercising Christ's power with him. There are many other verses particularly in **Revelation 2–3** which describe the rewards for those who 'overcome'.

STILL INTERESTED...?

The following list suggests some books written about the meaning and significance of the Christ's Passion. This may be a helpful place to start if you would like to investigate Jesus' death and the themes surrounding the cross in more depth.

Six Hours one Friday – Max Lucardo

Who Moved the Stone – Frank Morison

The Passion of Jesus Christ: Fifty Reasons Why He Came to Die – John Piper

The Cross of Christ – John Stott

Making Sense of the Cross – Alister McGrath

The Cross of Jesus – Leon Morris

The Death of Christ – James Denney

Connecting with the Heart of God
by Charles Price and Elizabeth McQuoid

Charles Price's commentary digs deep into the letter to the Hebrews and opens up the world of these first-century believers to us, helping to bridge the gap between the world of the Bible and our own.

Hebrews was written to address some of the fundamental misunderstandings about Jesus that the Jewish people had. The author is writing to correct their ignorance of who Christ was and to explain how Jesus Christ completes and fulfils Israel's history, Israel's law, Israel's ceremonial rituals and Israel's priesthood. This is a readable and incisive look at an essential book of the New Testament.

Additional material includes questions, discussion points, ideas for actions and further study.

Suitable for individual or group use.

'A practical and heart-warming introduction to Hebrews' profoundly encouraging message.' Jonathan Lamb, Langham Partnership International

Charles Price is the Senior Pastor of The Peoples Church in Toronto, Canada. Prior to this he worked as Principal of Capernwray Bible School. He has preached in many parts of the world and has often written on discipleship and the Bible.

Elizabeth McQuoid earned her Master of Divinity in America. She writes for a number of Christian publications.

ISBN: 1-85078-579-1

Available from your local Christian bookshop or www.WesleyOwen.com

King of Heaven, Lord of Earth: Colossians
by Steve Brady and Elizabeth McQuoid

'Therefore, as God's chosen people, holy and dearly loved, clothe yourselves with compassion, kindness, humility, gentleness and patience.' Colossians 3:12

Keswick speaker Steve Brady examines the book of Colossians, one of Paul's most readable letters. Written with his trademark searching insight and humour, it will unlock the book of Colossians in all its glory. Topics covered include growing in Christian maturity, how to keep away from deceptive teaching, living out God's standards in the community and the sufficiency of Christ.

Additional material includes questions, discussion points, ideas for actions and further study

Suitable for individual or group use

'A book that unwraps the message of Colossians and places it slap bang in the middle of our 21st century world.' Ian Coffey, Mutley Baptist Church, Plymouth

'Few people are able to communicate theological truth in a way that "grounds" it into our everyday life, as Steve Brady. I enthusiastically commend it.' John Glass, Elim

'Biblical, lively, practical, creative…a terrific resource.' Alistair Begg, Parkside Church, USA

Steve Brady studied at London Bible College, before serving in Baptist and Free Evangelical pastorates in Buckinghamshire, Leicester, East London and Bournemouth. He is currently the Principal of Moorlands College.

Elizabeth McQuoid earned her Master of Divinity in America. She writes for several Christian publications.

ISBN: 1-85078-481-7

Available from your local Christian bookshop or www.WesleyOwen.com

Turning Points
by Vaughan Roberts

Cinema and Sentiment: Film's Challenge to Theology
by Clive Marsh

Is there meaning to life?

Is human history a random process going nowhere?

Or is it under control – heading towards a goal, a destination?

And what about my life? Where do I fit into the grand scheme of things?

These are topical questions in any age, but perhaps particularly so in a largely disillusioned postmodern era such as ours. Vaughan Roberts addresses these questions and others as he looks at what the Bible presents as the 'turning points' in history, from creation to the end of the world.

This book does not read like a normal history book. No mention is made of great battles and emperors of whom we learnt at school. It will not help you pass exams or score extra marks in a pub quiz.

It aims to do something far more important, to help you see history as God sees it, so that you might fit in with his plans for the world.

'Racy and profound, brilliant and biblical, this book is a powerful apologetic and magnet to Jesus Christ.' Michael Green, Adviser in Evangelism to the Archbishops of Canterbury and York

Vaughan Roberts is Rector of St Ebbe's Church, Oxford. He has worked extensively with students and is a frequent speaker at University Christian Unions, and at conventions such as Word Alive and Keswick. He is a keen sportsman.

ISBN: 1-85078-336-5

Available from your local Christian bookshop or www.WesleyOwen.com

What do films do to people?

What do people do with films?

All film-watching happens within a cultural context. Exploring cinema-going as leisure activity and by comparing film-watching with worship, Clive Marsh demonstrates aspects of the religious function of film-watching in Western culture. Through a variety of case-studies, including a look at the films of Robin Williams and the Coen brothers, Marsh's study shows how film-watching as a regular practice contributes to the shaping of human living.

Engaging with rapidly changing social and religious behaviour patterns in Western culture, Cinema and Sentiment suggests a need to recover a positive sense of 'sentiment', both in theology and film. In his final chapter he offers to church leaders, students of theology and film studies, and all those with an interest in contemporary culture some very practical suggestions

'Marsh is right! Popular movies do more than mindlessly entertain or illustrate truth already known...By considering the affective nature of the reader/viewer, Cinema and Sentiment explores the central point of connection between theology and film.' Professor Robert K. Johnston, Author of Reel Spirituality

ISBN: 1-84227-274-8

Available from your local Christian bookshop or www.WesleyOwen.com